Color Nature
Easy Coloring Book For Adults
ColorFun
PUBLISHING
I0788965

Coloring Tips
For You

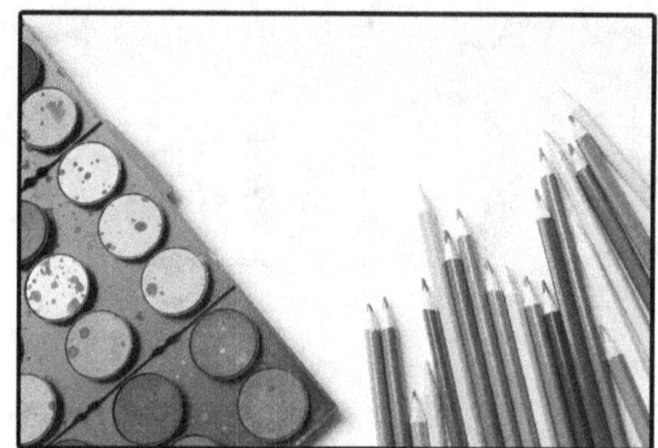

Experiment different tools for coloring:
crayons, colored pencils, markers, fine tip pens, pastels, etc.
You can even mix different tools on images to see what works best for you.
Remember the spirit: Have Fun!

Before you start, test your tool on the coloring test page.
This little move will make sure a great start on your coloring work.

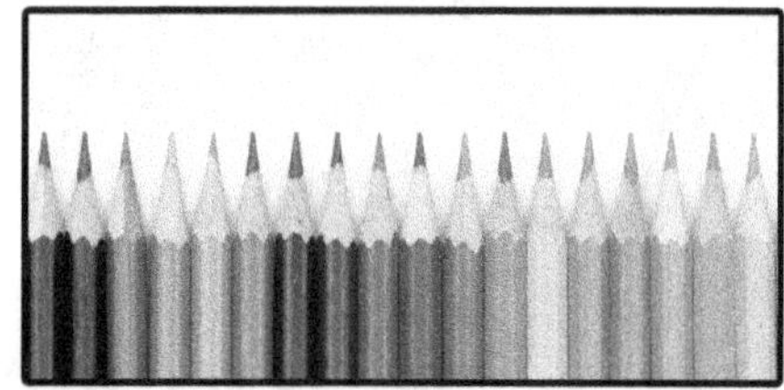

When using colored pencils, make sure they are sharp so that you can cover small areas or fine details with ease.

When using colored pencils, crayons or pastels, start out light!
You can always go back and darken your colors.

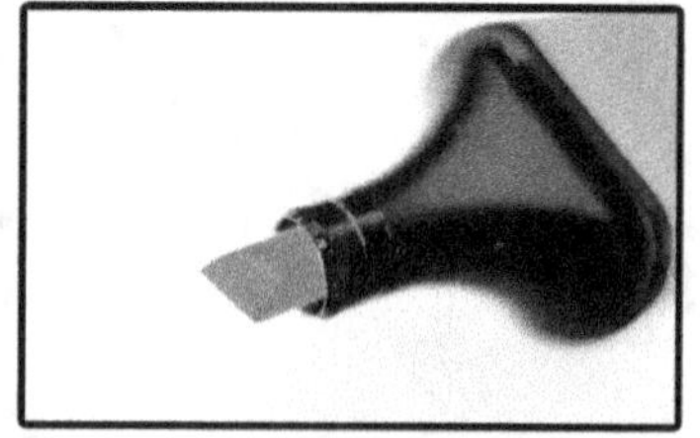

If you're using markers, it's highly recommended that you slide a thin paper or cardstock behind the pages you're working on. This tip is to prevent bleed-through.

Follow your instinct! You can start on any image of your choice and pick up any color you feel like at that particular moment for your coloring work.
Make sure it's a precious process that allows inner talk!

Perfection is NOT the goal! Enjoy coloring and let your creativity go wild.
After finishing this coloring book, go back and see how your creativity has evolved over the images.

HAVE A GREAT TIME COLORING!

This Book Belongs To:

Color Test Page

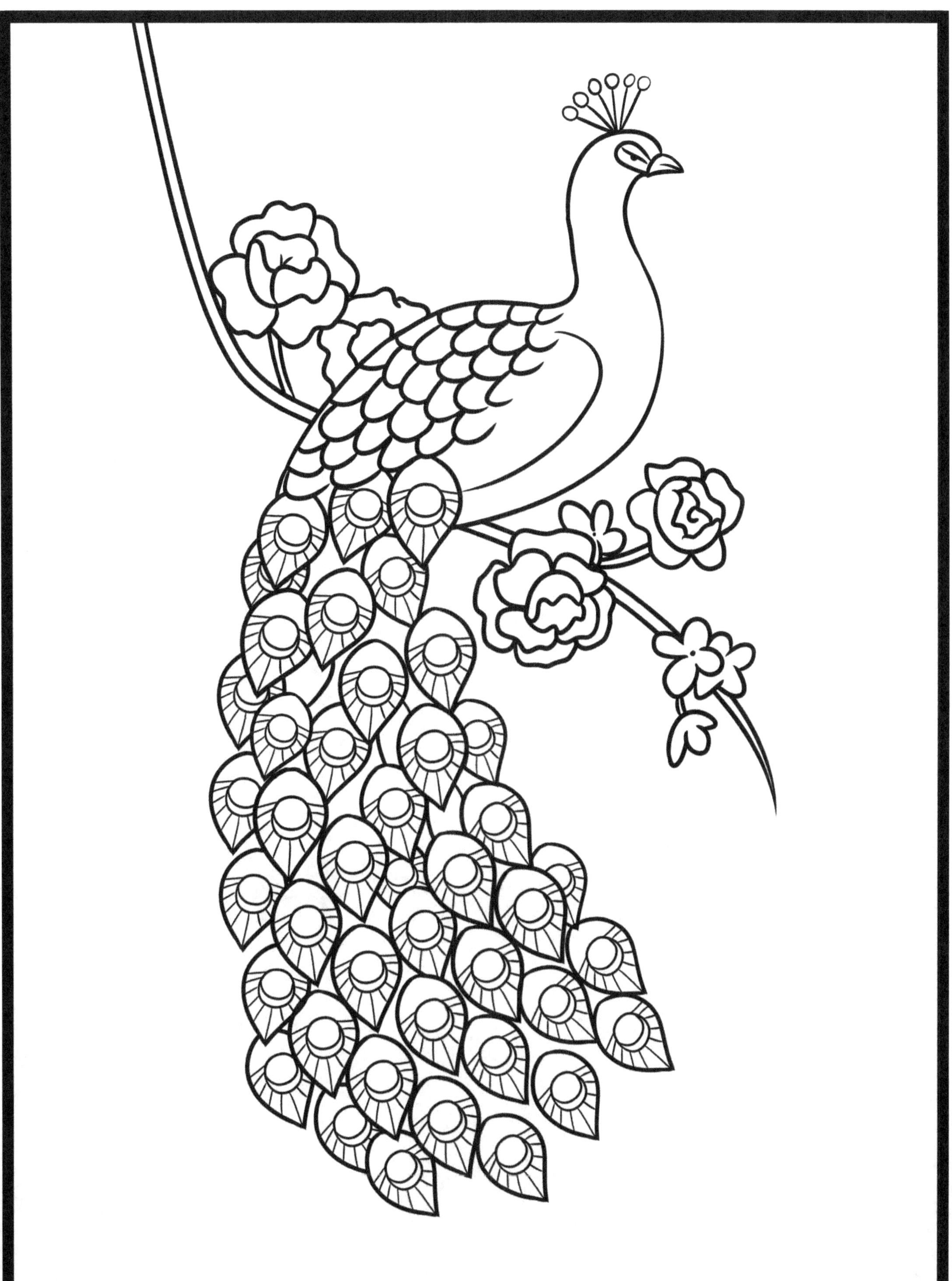

Hey, it's not finished yet!

How's your coloring journey?
Do you have fun with this coloring book?
Friends or families you gave this book to like this book?

As fellow colorists, we really want to know your thoughts on this book.
With your feedback, we'll be able to bring you more surprise with our
next books.

So, PLEASE HELP!

Help leaving helpful comments and rating on the website where you
found us.
Your comments and rating would definitely benefit others.

Meanwhile, you can share your work with us!
By sending your work to colorfunpublishing@gmail.com, you'll get FREE
digital copy of this coloring book.

That means, you can re-work on some of your favorite pages again!

Thank you again, and look forward to seeing your fantastic
coloring work!

Need More Fun?

CHECK OUT WHAT'S NEW WITH COLOR FUN PUBLISHING

Scan Now !
for More Book Info